STEP UP YOUR GAME

Overcoming Self-Doubt and
Believe in Your Ability to Lead Others

Sarita Wesley, Ph.D. LMSW

DEDICATION

This book is dedicated to the memory of my father,
Charles "The Godfather" Wesley, whose
lovingkindness, family values, and support
encouraged me to find the leader within me.

ACKNOWLEDGMENTS

First and foremost, I want to thank God for instilling in me the strength and stamina to write my first book. To my children, Tayler and Jordan, thank you for your patience and unconditional love. It is because of you that I have taken every opportunity to better myself and hope that you will do the same for your children. To my mother and role model Eula Wesley, thank you for setting the example. You taught me how to be an independent woman and supported me each step of the way. I am truly blessed to have a loving mother like you. To my sister Elaine, who saw the writing on the wall long before I did—I thank you for your support. To my close friends/sisters, thank you for always being there and supporting me no matter the circumstance. My college coach, Edwin Arnzen, I thank you for teaching me how to win at this game called life. We will always be family.

TABLE OF CONTENTS

Chapter 1: You Know What You Know   1

Chapter 2: Building Your Muscles   15

Chapter 3: Learn, Change, Relearn, and Repeat   25

Chapter 4: You Are What You Do   31

Chapter 5: Pack Your Bags and Grow with Me   39

Chapter 6: When the Going Gets Tough   47

Chapter 7: Like-Minded People   59

Chapter 8: Can People Relate to You?   73

Chapter 9: Look Inside Yourself   87

References   95

About the Author   97

Thank You For Reading My Book!   99

Chapter 1

You Know What You Know

"The pessimist complains about the wind. The optimist expects it to change. The leader adjusts the sails."

—John Maxwell

Realizing that you're a leader can sometimes be as clear as milk. And if you are honest with yourself, you've demonstrated leadership qualities for quite some time, but never truly accepted the calling for several reasons. Sometimes, that D word just sits out there like a sore thumb. Yes, I'm talking about the word DOUBT. It's one thing for someone else to doubt us, but when we doubt our own capabilities, we're really putting the nail in our own casket. Now, doubt may exist for several reasons, and that's okay as long as you don't stay in there and start to recognize your greatness. For starters, you may feel like you don't have the credentials to lead. However, I challenge you to look at all the

1

people in your life whom you consider to be leaders. I bet they may have just as many credentials as you, or maybe one more or one less. Also, a lack of skills could be another reason why you don't see yourself as a leader. You may feel like you don't have knowledge and the skill set to interpret and translate actions into outcomes. Moreover, you may feel intimidated by people who have tenure in the company and can do the job with their eyes closed, or you feel like you don't belong due to your ethnicity, upbringing, or socioeconomic background. And the list, I'm sure, can go on and on. Truth be told, if you asked a leader if any of these factors matter, they may tell you that they do. But they'll probably tell you that every leader has to overcome some type of barrier or apprehension that, in large part, contributed to them not only accepting the role of a leader but also becoming a successful leader, at that.

If you really think about it, you've probably been a leader as far back as you can remember. Discovering and accepting the fact that you're a leader can be scary, and you may not want to accept it. When we compare ourselves to great leaders, I think we envision a person sitting at the head of conference room table, wearing a nice dress or suit, who articulates every word correctly and appears to have it all together, right? Unfortunately, that's not the case. Leaders should present in a certain manner. But trust me, underneath the suit and tie and fancy words there also lies some form of apprehension or shortcomings. What I'm trying to say is that effective leaders have the same struggles and feelings about growing themselves as leaders as you do. They're just packaged differently.

It's great to be recognized as a leader. I mean, you can help the company and other employees meet goals and help others grow, or maybe you can't. It depends on the type of leader you are. I'll never forget, while teaching a business course, I asked the entire class if they thought they were a leader. Of course, everyone gave various responses, but one student stated, "I'm not a leader." When I asked her why she felt she wasn't a leader, she responded by stating, "I just don't think I can lead." My reply to her was, "I'm not sure about that, but we'll see." For some reason, I saw strengths in this student as she spoke about her profession and personal experiences. Through the course, the student emerged as the leader in the class and on her team. By the end of the course, I posed the exact same question about leadership to that student and she stated, "I think I've become more of a leader after realizing the extent of my job responsibilities, the essentialness of my role, and my ability to hold others accountable." The actions of the student identified her skills and capableness of growing as a leader.

Like this student, you may have had experiences shed light on your leadership potential that soon morphed it into dynamic leadership skills, making you realize that you were pretty darn good at your craft. Just like the student who didn't understand the value of her role at work or underestimated her skills, you, too, can change your outlook and willingly accept the challenge of becoming a well-respected leader.

ASSESSING THE PAST

As a little girl growing up in St. Louis, Missouri, I was a leader as far back as I can remember. On my neighborhood street, I played all the games kids loved to play at the time: kickball, dodgeball, jump rope, tag, hide-and-seek. I always was the bossiest, ran the fastest, and wanted to be first when participating in all activities. Some people today would probably say I was a little bit of a bully because I was bossy, but reflecting on that time, I'd like to think of myself as simply being assertive.

I came up with ideas for activities to do for the day, which mostly involved playing sports. For some reason, everyone would go along with my ideas. I had the luxury of starting kindergarten when I was four years old, and I walked to school, which was around the corner from my house, by myself with an air of self-confidence for someone who was just four years old. Some days, I would ride to school with a neighbor, and she and I would race to see who sat on the side of the car that allowed us to exit the car and enter the school first. Of course, I would win every race, and my friend would get upset and cry, but it didn't matter to me because I wanted to be the winner.

Around the seventh grade, I fell in love with the game of basketball. Although I was smaller than most girls playing at the time (I was only five-foot-three) I played with a lot of heart. I played so well that I was the starting point guard on my high school varsity team as a sophomore. I was nowhere near the best player, but I played the point guard position, so that meant I handled the ball, ran the offense, and even became a defensive specialist. I played so well in high school that a newspaper called me the best point guard that came out of St. Louis in my senior year. This led to me accepting a scholarship for one of the top Division II women's basketball programs in the nation at Southeast Missouri State University. During those four years, my leadership skills really began to evolve—although, sometimes I wonder if I really had a choice. My coach, Edwin Arnzen, was a no-nonsense-type coach who pushed me beyond measure. He constantly rode my ass, but, at the same time, continually explained the importance of my role as the point guard of the team. Many times, I felt defeated by his constructive criticism, but not once did I ever give up. I really tried to understand what he wanted from me and did my best to meet his expectations. I didn't understand, at the time, that he was preparing me to be a leader, not only on the court but also in life.

All matters weren't always black and white, and lessons were learned in mostly the gray areas. One time, we lost a game, and instead of assessing the game to understand why we lost and what I could have done better, I decided to go to a party on campus. Somehow, my coach found out I had attended the party and addressed the issue with me. My initial response was, "Coach, it was only a party." However, he questioned my leadership on the team because he thought the loss should have impacted me in such a way that I should have processed my mistakes and what the team needed to do to turn things around. The next game we played was against the number 10 ranked team in the nation, and I had a very solid game. When a reporter interviewed me after the game, I told them, in my novelty, that Coach Arnzen questioned my ability to be a collegiate player, and that night I showed him that I was. When my senior year arrived, we had more freshmen on the team than any other year. Having such a young team meant that upperclassmen had to help them adjust to sports on the collegiate level. I always did my part and supported and encouraged everyone to give their all. I guess you can say I adjusted the sails. I thought of the team as my team, and took great ownership, held teammates accountable, and had a solid understanding of how important each person's role was on the team. By the end of my senior year, the team was on ESPN, playing for the national championship, only to come up seven points short of the win. Many years after the season, I had a conversation with Coach Arnzen and told him, as we reminisced, that the center on our team, Jerri Wiley, led us that year. He replied, "No, Rita," as he often called me, "Jerri was the most athletic player, but you were the leader on our team."

A plethora of research debates whether a person is born a leader or taught to be a leader, and this book doesn't discuss those points. However, reflecting on my evolution as leader helped me understand that, while I didn't always embody a number of skills to be a leader, people in my life saw something in me and helped shape and mold the potential until it actually came to fruition. I cannot lead people in my place of employment exactly like my basketball team, but, in many ways, I do because the game of basketball and the game of life are very relatable.

Are you a leader? Of course, that's a question that no one can answer for you. But be open and assess your life so you may have a better understanding of the leader who lies within.

"Leaders are made; they're not born. They're made by hard effort, which is the price which all of us must pay to achieve any goal that is worthwhile."

—Vince Lombardi

ACTION STEPS:

1. Access your life experiences so you can identify where the seed of leadership was planted in your life.

2. Evaluate your personal and professional goals. Where do you want to be in life in the next three to five years?

3. Evaluate your ethics and integrity. Do your words and actions align with one another?

STEP UP YOUR GAME

ACCEPTING THE ROLE

---

*"If your actions inspire others to dream more, learn more,
do more and become more, you are a leader."*

—John Quincy Adams

I've come to believe too many of us were lured and not led into leadership roles.

Leadership is a calling on your life, but are you willing to accept the call? Are you willing to remove doubt that has impeded your growth and to begin to focus on excelling as a leader? If you want to earn more money, get promoted, move from a cubicle to an office in the right-wing of the floor, or gain more power and influence, then your only option is to move from being an independent contributor to a leader of people. The transition into leadership absolutely requires new talents. You can grow them, but only if you're aware of them. Ask other leaders what they struggle with. What have they mastered? What still surprises them about the role. When you're clear about what your team or others need from you, assess which of your strengths still apply and which skills you need to develop. You might be surprised. If you're willing to acknowledge you need to develop new skills and even leave some successful ones behind, you're going to be a stellar leader. Once you realize that others see that you're capable of being a leader, you must be willing to embrace it. Well, one may ask, "What do people see in me?" That's a perfectly fair question. You may think of a leader as someone who is very charismatic and gives an hour-long presentation in front of thousands of participants. In real life, leadership is a much quieter trait, but, somehow, you really make a difference in the lives of others.

We've all been there, at one time or another. Some days, you want to just lie in bed. You want to stay there, eat your meals there, and go back to sleep. Nevertheless, you push it aside and force yourself out of bed because you have responsibilities. You have people counting on you and things to get done that won't finish themselves. This is called being responsible. Leaders need be responsible when no one else wants to be.

All leaders know that leading can be a daunting task, and some blatantly deny taking on additional responsibilities. I remember working at a health clinic that needed a manager to help lead the clinical dynamics of the business. The clinic had people who were well qualified to take the position, but when asked why they didn't want the position, most stated, "The job has too much responsibility." Admittedly, I was taken aback more by this response than by the lack of interest in the position. If you don't want to be responsible for outcomes and helping others grow, then a leadership position may not be in your best interest because they go hand in hand. On the other hand, if you're willing to take on extra responsibilities, volumes of new knowledge can be acquired.

While working in a team setting with peers, my supervisor asked who would like to ensure that the deadlines for certain tasks were completed on time and to provide an update about the progress of the team weekly. Of course, I didn't immediately volunteer. For starters, I knew my professional plate was full and my personal plate wasn't lagging too far behind. At that time, I wasn't in a leadership position, but I decided that this would be the perfect opportunity to highlight some of my skills or make a complete blunder of myself. I prayed that the outcomes would present as expected and, at the end of the day, I would still be employed. I welcomed the challenge to take on extra responsibility, and it paid off. I ensured that all teammates completed their specific tasks and provided weekly updates. At the end of the project, my supervisor requested that I present the findings of the project to executive-level leaders. Well, that wasn't part of the plan, but I had to roll with the punches because I couldn't turn back. My heart dropped for a mere second, but I quickly gathered my thoughts once again and told myself that presenting the information is a great way to share my organizational and presentation skills. Also, it was a great opportunity for leaders to put a face with my name and for me to shine.

Throughout my professional journey, I've learned that accepting the fact that you're a leader doesn't always have to be a cumbersome task, but can actually help you build your knowledge, skill set, and self-confidence, and allow other employees to become familiar with your work and ability to lead initiatives.

ACTION STEPS:

1. Confront your doubts. Accept the fact that you have leadership qualities.

2. Step out on faith. God will not place more on you than you can bear.

3. Shine in the light. Take on additional responsibilities to help build your skills.

UNDERSTANDING PEOPLE

*"He who knows others is wise;
he who knows himself is enlightened."*

—Lao Tzu

The textbook definition of leadership is: "The ability of an individual to lead or guide other individuals, teams, or an entire organization." Without a doubt, we understand that leadership is about leading people. However, people come from all walks of life (i.e., different ethnicity, values, upbringing, education, and socioeconomic status). The point I'm making is that everyone lives their life differently from one another, so how does a leader get everyone motivated and moving in the same direction?

For example, a rowing crew that's off rhythm will go in circles and never reach the finish line, let alone win. To be an efficient team, all members must row in perfect sync with one another, moving the boat quickly in the same direction. Well, the same rule applies to your organization. Often, business leaders set goals that are never achieved because the company's team members are not lined up to work toward the same goals. A leader needs to interact with their followers, peers, seniors, and others to accomplish their goals. To gain their support, a leader must be able to understand and motivate them. To do this, they must understand human behavior, the common qualities of all human beings, and that people behave according to certain principles of human nature.

Often, I witness leaders who are just focused on the numbers and metrics of a business. Now, I'm not stating that the data isn't important, but as leaders, we must continuously keep in the fore of our thoughts that people are not merely mechanisms to ensure metrics and targets are met. I believe the quote by John Maxwell states it best, "People don't care about how much you know until they know how much you care." As leaders, we must remember that employees are not simply widget makers, and want to feel valued. It doesn't mean that employees shouldn't be held accountable for outcomes, but leaders must be mindful of the balancing act it takes to ensure people feel valued at the same time. When you understand human behavior, you'll have a better chance of galvanizing the troops and getting them to buy into your vision and follow you. Understand, human behavior isn't about knowing the intricacies of a person's life; it simply boils down to a few factors.

People want to feel that you care about them as a whole, instead of just as an employee. This means you ask them a few personal questions about themselves, such as their children, future goals, thoughts on some current societal topics, etc. People want to be engaged. If, as a leader, you only talk about numbers, goals, and outcomes, people won't feel connected, but more like a number. When feelings like this set in, productivity and continuity can be lost, and turnover will soon follow.

Case in point, when I worked for a social service agency, the manager was very nice but primarily focused on hitting the daily goals of the division. This was perfectly okay, but she didn't show employees that she valued their efforts. She never took the time to have one-on-one meetings to get a better understanding of her team members. The only time they would have extensive conversations was when something went wrong, so, of course, that conversation always came across as being punitive. After three months, several team members knew this wasn't a place they wanted to be employed at and began looking for other employment opportunities. As a leader, your concern for your people is important. If you keep the lines of communication open between you and your employees, you can't help but build relationships with your employees. An employee with an unresolved problem won't work to full potential.

By observing human behavior, you can gain the knowledge you need to better understand yourself and other people. You can learn why people act and react in certain ways. You can learn how to identify the various types of behavior and needs of people, but, most importantly, how to counter those behaviors, if necessary. Also, you can learn how to influence the behavior of people so that they can see how meeting the needs of the organization is vital. The organizational goals, policies, and outcomes will always be present, but as Maya Angelou wrote, "People may forget what you said, but they will never forget how you made them feel."

ACTION STEPS:

1. Take time to get to know your employees. Discover what makes them tick.

2. Make deposits into individuals to garner withdrawals from individuals.

CHAPTER 2

BUILDING YOUR MUSCLES

"Courage is not the absence of fear, but rather the judgment that something else is more important than fear."

—Ambrose Redmoon

When I work out and challenge myself to lift heavier weights, my muscles become sore, but I know that I've worked them to the point that they'll grow. If you never work your muscles, over time, they'll become weak and flabby. Well, the same principle holds true about leadership. If you don't work hard or have systems in place to help meet goals and objectives, the muscles will atrophy.

When you try something new or attempt to do something that has never been done before, I can guarantee that many will doubt you, try to dissuade you, and perhaps even chuckle at your naïveté. You, too, will have your own doubts, from

STEP UP YOUR GAME

time to time, but don't let them get you down. You must have the courage to overcome your doubters and detractors. A job title means very little if the hard work doesn't follow. Leadership isn't about basking in the glory of the position (and title) that has been bestowed upon you, but, rather, concentrating on the responsibilities and impact that come with that title.

Most of the time, when I asserted myself as a leader, I didn't even realize the level of courage it took to lead. It was an action that was more natural than anything else. Over time, when I realized and accepted the fact that I was a leader, I became more confident in my leadership ability. Looking back at the days of playing collegiate sports, it took courage to play in front of thousands of fans who supported the team, direct my teammates, and run the offense on the floor. As I moved into my professional career, it took courage to establish my goals and push myself to not be just an average employee. At the same time, I had the courage to take risks and not be afraid to fail. Courage is more than being able to stick your chest out when everything is running smoothly. Becoming courageous is when you come up short but refuse to let that incident define you and, instead, you willingly take on other tasks or another outlook and create a multitude of small victories. First, the courage to not give up is something to admire, in and of itself. I believe that instances of failures and small victories are some of the most enlightening times in a person's life.

I was a program director for a nonprofit when the findings from an audit were subpar. As the leader, I knew I had to take the hit on the chin. A few areas needed to be adjusted, and I remember feeling like I had failed, but just for a moment. No matter the outcome, I had to pull myself up by my bootstraps and lead like never before. When things don't pan out the way you intended, it seems like that's when the brightest light is beaming on you, and others are sitting back wondering how you're going to respond. Effective leaders apportion credit where it is due, which fosters morale and a team ethos. Similarly, when a mistake is made, a leader must have courage and face up to the ultimate responsibility. When the leader takes responsibility, team members are shielded from finger pointing and allowed to get on with the task at hand. This is exactly what I did. I addressed the errors, developed new processes, encouraged the team to work together to correct the errors, and emphasized how we would be prepared for the follow-up audit.

If I hadn't had the courage to take responsibility for the results of the audit and reassess where I could have done things differently, that wouldn't have allowed the team to refocus on the needed adjustments. Taking responsibility for failure isn't a good feeling, but having the courage to own mistakes and correct them speaks to one's ability to build trust with the team and effectively lead.

When I was in college, living in the dormitory, we had a curfew when company had to be out of the dorm. During my sophomore year in college, a basketball recruit was visiting, and we had a small gathering in my dorm room. We ordered pizza, and before I knew it, time had passed and the visitors were in the dorm after visiting hours. We were kind of noisy, so the hall monitor knocked on the door to tell us to quiet down. She noted that we had violated curfew. She informed me that she was going to write me up, and the only thing I could do was take responsibility. The first thing I did the next morning was call my basketball coach and explain what happened. My coach said, "Thank you for informing me, Rita; I appreciate the notice." He later told me in person that when I informed him first, it indicated that I took responsibility for my actions and was maturing as a leader. Of course, I never thought of my actions as a sign of leadership; I simply thought I was letting my coach know that I had gotten in trouble before anyone else told him. But, in the bigger scheme of things, I was building my leadership muscle.

If you want to be a leader, you must be willing to stand for something. You must go out on a limb and profess and practice your belief in someone, something, and/or some cause. Rather than sitting idly by and doing nothing, leadership demands that you put yourself out there to be a passionate advocate for whatever you're supporting or defending. When you extend yourself, you must be prepared and courageous enough to take shots and criticism from those who don't support you or your cause, but if you believe in yourself, others will, too.

ACTION STEPS:

1. Work harder to become stronger.

2. Good things come to those who work hard.

3. Fall down seven times; stand up eight.

DON'T BE AFRAID TO MAKE MISTAKES

---

*"Mistakes are always forgivable
if one has the courage to admit them."*

—Bruce Lee

Everyone—yes, including you—will never be perfect in this lifetime. However, to grow in any capacity, failure or mistakes must happen.

- Don't run from your mistakes.

- Don't try to spin your mistakes.

- Don't try to pass the burden of your mistakes onto someone else's shoulders.

- Don't make a mistake worse by not owning it or trying to sweep it under the rug. When you do that, you're just building a house on sand.

Some of you may disagree with that outlook, but it seems that when you fail or err in various roles in life, as a leader, you should be able to:

- Assess what you did incorrectly.

- Figure out what you could have done differently.

- Admit your fault or failure to yourself and your team/employees.

- Share how you plan on correcting the mistake and what can be done to mitigate the matter from occurring again.

When you take sole responsibility for your actions/mistakes, you allow others to see that you're human and how you rebounded from the mistake and "righted the wrong." Also, I've learned that it's awfully difficult for someone to refute a person who takes ownership of their mistake. When I worked as an administrator at a clinic, I once overbooked new clients who needed treatments on a certain day. When a new admit starts services, a lot of paperwork must be completed. During the enrollment process, a few nurses began to complain about the admissions and the amount of extra work they had to complete. I overheard them talking and informed them that I inadvertently scheduled too many patients for admissions on the same day and explained how it happened. In short, I didn't effectively communicate with the office assistant who typically handles all admissions. After the dust cleared, I met with the team to discuss the situation, and, at the same time, developed a plan of action that I thought would avoid similar situations from occurring again. The team liked and agreed on the plan, and we moved forward from that point. I could have easily made excuses, blamed my office assistant, and/or simply ignored the complaints of the nurses. How cool would that have been? Not very, and it could have tarnished the view my teammates had of me.

There's nothing more cowardly than someone consciously making a mistake but refusing to admit their fault when confronted. This is usually when you can, and will, lose respect for them. Denial has never gotten anyone anywhere in life. Admitting your mistake won't suddenly render you to be less as a human being, or anything of the sort. If you really want to save any relationship, even if it's just the one with yourself, lose the ego and be up front about it.

The strongest and best thing you can do for the sake of yourself and others is taking responsibility. The same way we take pride in an award we've won or a position we hold, we must also take ownership of our mishaps. Confronting your mistake head on will allow you to accept the error and move forward in a healthy manner.

So you're not caught off guard, just know that "stuff happens." Well-laid plans don't always turn out exactly the way you would have anticipated. A sale that was one signature away from being finalized falls apart at the last minute. One missed detail takes a project down the wrong path, and it then costs a significant amount to bring it back on track. The leadership journey is fraught with unexpected challenges and unknown landmines, and sometimes even the smallest misstep by a leader can result in financial and reputational loss. I'm not mentioning these facts to deter you, of course, but, rather, how you respond to mistakes will determine whether you're a leader or a manager. At the end of the day, leaders unequivocally accept full responsibility for mistakes. Sure, other people and other factors may have contributed to the error, but, ultimately, leaders admit accountability and take full ownership for the missteps. Leaders don't blame, point fingers, or deflect accountability. They own up to the mistake and apologize.

"It's not how we make mistakes,
but how we correct them that defines us."

—Rachel Wolchin

ACTION STEPS:

1. Admit your mistakes, no matter the consequence.

2. Successes and failures are bound to occur, but how you respond is the key.

Chapter 3

Learn, Change, Relearn, and Repeat

"Leadership and learning are indispensable to each other."

—**John Fitzgerald Kennedy**

Skills, knowledge, and more skills are what it takes to be an effective leader. Stated another way, practice makes perfect, and leaders should always be willing to challenge and enlighten themselves to continuously grow, and not just for the sake of harboring what they've learned, but to be able to share it with others so they may enhance their skills, too. Smart leaders know what they don't know. Learning is a constant process throughout your professional life, and it doesn't stop when you've become any type of leader. Make sure to never stop looking for opportunities for professional development and to pass on the wisdom you've learned to your people.

During my freshman year in college, I wasn't the starting point guard. I received a lot of playing time, but I had so much to learn before I could lead the team on the floor. The upperclassmen were far more talented than I. Because I wanted to get better, I listened and observed the techniques of the guards who were more experienced. Countless times, I got knocked down. My coach yelled and embarrassed me, but I remained open to learning and becoming a better point guard and leader on the team. After my freshman year, I was in line for the starting position. However, there was one small caveat: the coach was bringing in another point guard recruit to play the same position. I met the recruit when she visited the campus. She was a junior college transfer and told me she was going to be the new point guard. When she made that statement, I cringed because I knew that was supposed to be my position. When I went home for the summer, I worked very hard on my game. I played with the guys in my neighborhood to help strengthen my toughness and endurance. I worked tirelessly on my jump shot and jogged every day to be sure I was conditioned. When I returned to college in the fall, the recruit was now my teammate, and we battled on the floor daily. During preseason, which entailed conditioning and scrimmaging daily, I evolved as the "starting" point guard, and the recruit who stated she was going to be in the starting lineup quit the team.

The point I'm making is that, because I was open to learning from others who had been in my position and worked my butt off during the off-season, I eventually evolved as the leader on the team. Similarly, when you want to move out of your cubicle and into the corner office, you have to arm yourself with skills and knowledge so that you'll be prepared to tackle what's in front of you. Based on my experience, ascertaining knowledge by researching leadership is important, but applying what you've read is where the rubber meets the road and when learning from experience begins.

When assessing your leadership capabilities, you must consider variables that may contribute to your leadership style. A few of the variables may be upbringing, culture, environment, socioeconomic background, education, life lessons, etc. No matter what the contributing factors may be, a leader must be mindful to always work on enhancing their craft of leading others. When my supervisor and coworkers on various jobs observed or assessed my leadership style and provided feedback, it was mostly positive. The feedback meant that I was perfectly imperfect, but I listened to it, owned it, and applied it. I focused on areas of improvement so I could continue to grow. I dialogued with people in higher positions and learned tremendously about various management theories. Additionally, I learned about the latest books and authors. Three of my favorite authors are Stephen Covey, John Maxwell, and Maya Angelou. These authors shared various adages and mantras that I consciously exhibit in my daily actions. As I mentioned in another chapter, one of my favorite adages by John Maxwell is, "People don't care about how much you know until they know how much you care." This adage helps me focus daily on my team first and outcomes second, because I first must recognize that goals and/or outcomes are met by team members who are literally on the front line. More importantly, I first recognize that they're human beings, and treat them with respect and dignity. Most importantly, I value them far beyond just being employees, and it makes a difference in the effort they employ in helping the team meet its goals and outcomes.

While working with a newly-hired clinical lead who had a wealth of clinical knowledge, I was very eager to learn from her so I could enhance my clinical knowledge. When she arrived, she met with the team, shared her clinical knowledge, and established some tasks that the team needed to complete. Because she was new to the team, there was a little pushback, but the team still completed the tasks. One issue needed to be troubleshot right away, and she met with the team on a Friday to develop and implement a strategy. As part of the leadership team, she and I were typically off on weekends, but when I woke up Saturday morning, the clinical lead and the issue we were working on crossed my mind. I replayed all the steps we had taken to implement the strategy, and then it hit me. The clinical lead would continue to encounter pushback unless she showed that she valued the team members. I took the liberty to call her and asked if she had called the team to check on them. She hadn't. I explained to her that people want to feel valued and know that you care about them, so it would be good to call the team members, not only to see how the strategy implementation was going, but also to check on the team and make sure they were okay, personally. Also, if they needed anything, to let them know they could contact her and count on her for support. I informed her that, because she was new, it was of utmost importance that she gained buy-in from the team, and valuing people as individuals could make a difference. She said, "Well, what you're saying makes sense. I'll do it." Later that day, I received a text stating, "Thank you for contacting me and sharing your wisdom." Well, it wasn't really my wisdom, but knowledge I had learned from other leaders and employees in my daily life. Once a conscious and courageous effort to learn and grow as a leader are felt within the depth of your heart, you're on your way to growing as a leader, and the sky is the limit.

ACTION STEPS:

1. Seek knowledge and be open to learning from others.

2. Understand that learning is not a static but continuous process.

CHAPTER 4

YOU ARE WHAT YOU DO

"Setting an example is not the main means
of influencing others, it is the only means."

—Albert Einstein

L eadership is influence—nothing more and nothing less. If a person can influence another to take some course of action, they're a leader. So, you're probably asking yourself who you have influenced or the number of people you have influenced. Carl Jung stated, "You are what you do, not what you say you'll do," and it applies to how leaders are perceived when they lead. I was always told that a person's perception is their reality, and the only way it can be altered is if the person views something in a different light. Have you ever worked for a supervisor who, if not for their title, you couldn't tell if they were the leader or not? If so, the person may not be the best fit for a leadership position. Leading by example means that you must set and maintain certain standards, despite any given situation. For example, one of my employees disagreed with a decision I made and started to talk to others about the disagreement and how they didn't like me, etc. I had no idea that the team member felt the way they did, but my deputy director called a meeting with me and told me that conversation had taken place. We talked at length about my decision, which was very much aligned with the company's mission/vision and goals, and I informed my supervisor that I would follow up with the teammate to discuss the matter. At that point, I was livid, but more disappointed that I received the news from my supervisor rather than from the person who disagreed with my decision. I held my composure while speaking to my supervisor, but to be perfectly honest, I was furious. I was just hoping she didn't see the smoke shooting from my ears.

Nevertheless, I called a meeting with the team member to discuss their concerns. Initially, I didn't want to hear anything the person had to say because I knew I made a decision that was best for my team and the business. However, because I was the leader, I had to be mindful to keep my cool and practice active listening and patience. When the teammate entered my office, I greeted them and explained why we were meeting. I told them that I was informed that they disagreed with a decision I made. The teammate explained that they thought I was giving the team more work and didn't think it was fair. Now, I really wanted to say, "Why were you speaking negatively about me? I was really embarrassed because the deputy director brought the matter to my attention instead of you." I really wanted to read the teammate their Miranda rights, but I knew I had to use a different tactic. Before speaking to the team member, I had to gather my thoughts and really focus on the outcome I wanted. So, I focused on the concerns of the team member to show that I was interested in hearing their point of view. After gathering that information, I focused on explaining, in more depth, my rationale for the decision and how the new task would impact the organization and the segment of the population we served.

Next, I focused on how to help the person make the tasks manageable so they wouldn't seem so laborious. When the discussion ended, I didn't know if the person felt any different about me as a leader, but they had a better understanding of the task and responsibility associated with it. Could my approach have been different? Of course, it could have. But when you're a leader, sometimes you have to remove yourself from the equation and focus on the issue at hand. Whether or not the team member liked me was irrelevant, because that was a personal matter and we were in a professional setting. I had to focus on the professional aspect of the matter, which was the person completing their job responsibilities. I've learned that, to be an effective leader, you have to stay focused on the outcome because it's so easy to get bogged down with irrelevant matters that will easily make you lose focus. More importantly, I had to set the example and treat the person how I would want to be treated.

"The three most important ways to lead people are: by example... by example... by example."

—Albert Schweitzer

ACTION STEPS:

1. Remain professional at all times.

2. Establish and focus on achieving your outcomes.

TRUSTING IS BELIEVING

"Trust is built with consistency."

—Lincoln Chafee

There are several skills leadership should encompass. One of the most important skills is the ability to build trust with others. Have you ever tried befriending or working with someone you don't trust? It probably puts a real damper on the relationship, and may even impact how much effort you put into completing certain tasks. Well, the same holds true for you as a leader. If your employees don't trust you, they won't give you 100 percent of their effort and/or they may not respect you as a leader. Stephen Covey, a leadership guru, stated, "The first job of any leader is to inspire trust." Trust is confidence born of two dimensions: character and competence. Character includes your integrity, motive, and intent with people. Competence includes your capabilities, skills, results, and track record. Both dimensions are vital. Trust is a pinnacle of effective leadership—but it doesn't come with your title. Building trust as a leader and throughout your workforce is an ongoing process, and when trust is strong, employees thrive, and so does business.

What has worked for me repeatedly is my ability to be honest, transparent, and truthful with others, whether or not the other person likes what's being stated. While stating facts or being truthful, I'm always respectful. Aside from that point, one of the main steps I take is to communicate, communicate, communicate. You should always keep everyone apprised of updated news and changes as they occur, especially when employees' daily job tasks may be impacted. A bylaw I use is that my employees won't hear information from everyone else before they hear it from me. This doesn't happen at 100 percent, but it occurs more often than not. Leaders… this is a vital point! When people know that you're upfront and transparent, whether the information is positive or negative, these actions help build trust. To this point, I've spoken mostly about the leader-to-employee perspective of building trust, but leaders must also practice similar steps when addressing their supervisor. No one likes to be blindsided with news, unless you're notified that you're receiving a large increase in pay and a new car. How nice that would be! Leaders can help increase their trust by informing their supervisors when the numbers for the quarter are low or if someone is looking to transfer. Another valuable point is that, if your supervisor shares information with you, the same information doesn't come back to the leader via someone else. When another leader confides in you, it isn't because you're their best friend, but because they want to know if they can trust you. Therefore, the levels of communication work both ways, and so does building trust.

Another key aspect of building trust with employees is to follow through on what you say you're going to do. Said more simply, "Do as you say; say as you do." When people around you know that you're going to complete a task as planned or promised and you do it within a certain timeframe to the best of your ability, you are more apt to build trust. From another perspective, if you inform your employees that you're going to allow everyone one hour of compensation time a week to complete company training, then do just that, unless there are mitigating factors, but be sure to explain the mitigating factors.

Leaders also build trust when they empathize with employees and the employees know that they want the best for them. People are simply not widget makers; they're human and want to feel valued like everyone else. If a leader treats an employee like they're a number, the chances of building trust are zero to none. I make a point to always converse with employees about their families, their weekend plans, and family vacations. I remember the conversations we have in the break room and follow up with them later as a quick check-in to let them know I was listening and care. I want them to know that I genuinely care about them outside of just being an employee who helps the organization reach goals and outcomes. This doesn't mean that the deepest and darkest secrets are discussed, but personal information can be shared in such a way that professionalism is never compromised.

Building trust can help retain top talent and improve workplace culture. A high level of trust in the workplace makes for a much more fulfilling and enjoyable work experience that will pay off with improved employee productivity and overall engagement.

Action Steps:

1. Be the first to share and discuss information that impacts employees.

2. Dispel rumors and gossip.

3. Show that you care about others.

CHAPTER 5

PACK YOUR BAGS
AND GROW WITH ME

*"Before you are a leader, success is all about
growing yourself. When you become a leader,
success is all about growing others."*

—Jack Welch

A s you grow as a leader, your knowledge and skills should
grow, as well. A lot of times, people think leading is
about telling others what to do, getting the task completed,
high-fiving everyone afterwards to celebrate the success, and
then starting the cycle all over again. In large part, becoming
an effective leader is also about one's ability to grow others.
When leaders grow leaders, everyone is winning, especially
the organization. Leaders help bring out the best in others
and help them apply and develop their strengths to reach

their goals. These are the people who provide challenges and opportunities to help you go where you want to go. They're working to make a bigger pie where everyone can be successful.

I've worked for leaders who didn't like to share their knowledge and set others up to be successful because they were so worried about other people taking their position. If a leader has this type of mindset, they're not an effective leader and selfish. Leaders, no matter the position, carry some sort of power. However, leaders must realize that, when they share their power, (a) they help grow others, and (b) they expand their power. The growing of power occurs when you share your knowledge and it leads to someone else completing a task, but, at the same time, increases their ability to learn a new skill. When the person completes the task, they now understand how to do it, moving forward. The leader who assigned the task just needs to have oversight to ensure it was done correctly. This example highlights how a win-win situation occurs. Employees grow and the task is completed. If the actions are consistently repeated, the person can develop other skills that move their status upward in the organization.

As a program director, I supervised team leaders who, in return, directly supervised front-line staff. During one meeting, one team leader was slumped down in the chair with a mean look on her face, giving an impression that she didn't want to attend the meeting. During the meeting, I made eye contact with her, instead of addressing the issue in front of everyone. She recognized my cue, sat up straight, and engaged in the meeting. After the meeting, I discussed the matter with her and explained that, because she was a team leader, she had to set the example for her team. She had to remember that the energy she put into the team was the energy she would get out of the team. She agreed with my assessment, and since that time, the issue never had to be addressed again. In fact, she was promoted to a program director position, and I couldn't have been prouder of her. When she transitioned, she thanked me immensely for helping her grow as a leader and reminding her of the importance of being professional even when you don't want to be.

"I start with the premise that the function of leadership is to produce more leaders, not more followers."

—Ralph Nader

ACTION STEPS:

1. Share knowledge so others can grow.

2. Leaders grow leaders.

3. Dare to Be Different

"The best way a mentor can prepare another leader is to expose him or her to other great people."

—John C. Maxwell

When you can shine, take advantage of it, because if you don't, others will. This may very well mean taking on tasks that seem minute. But, on a larger scale, it provides an opportunity to showcase your talents. Amongst other things, it indicates that you're willing to take on additional responsibilities, something that some people shy away from because it's extra work.

Another important point is your presentation. How you present yourself to others is an indicator of how you want others to perceive you. Over the many years I've worked in various organizations, I have noted people who dress totally inappropriate for work. Leaders within an organization want someone who sets a good example for the company. This is why presentation is important. To better understand how you should present yourself, find someone you respect and admire and mimic their style. For example, my mentor, Barbara Davis, dressed exceptionally well. She wore nice business suits and carried herself in a professional manner at all times. When given the opportunity to work under her tutelage, she set the example and taught me of the importance of presentation.

When my college basketball team played for the Division II National Championship on ESPN, the ESPN commentator made the statement, "When she dribbles, Sarita Wesley goes in the opposite direction of the defense. If her person guarding goes to the right, she dribbles to the left." The dribble, as described by the commentator, was intended to give me space to pass, shoot, or continue dribbling the basketball. When I accepted the fact that I could be an effective leader, I applied a similar strategy. In short, I intentionally strove to be different from other employees, or traveled in a different direction. I didn't hang out in the break room, gossiping. I was very selective about whom I surrounded myself with at work. This didn't mean that I didn't socialize with others, it just meant that I did so at a distance. I'll never forget, during one of my employee evaluation meetings, my supervisor stated, "You know, I never hear your name in a negative light." It wasn't that I was perfect, but I saw the bigger picture and knew I wanted to grow within the organization, so I had to set the stage. No one was going to do it for me.

During meetings with brass level staff, I listened and observed who the players were, just like I did when I prepared against an opponent. You must know your opponent's strengths and weaknesses to be able to maneuver, challenge, and beat them. The concept of learning to be a leader is no different. Typically, organizations are structured with various levels of leadership, and if you want to grow, you must identify who the important people are, or the role they play within the organization. The players are the individuals who are in leadership positions; they hire and fire or hold some sort of weight in the organization. If you cannot present or directly communicate with executive leaders, there's always a dotted line that leads to them, and the dotted line is someone else who can vouch for your character and work ethic. Once you identify who the players are, you must learn how to be politically correct in all the steps you take. Being politically correct means that you don't overstep your boundaries and don't put others down for the sake of getting ahead. Actions like this will come back to bite you. I'm informing you to follow the chain of command, be respectful, follow the policies, watch who you keep in your circle, know when to laugh and when to be quiet and listen, don't be a know-it-all, and research information and share it.

Over the past several years, I've taken advantage of elevator rides to engage in conversations with upper-level leaders. What a perfect time to have small talk about the weather, the latest sport wins-losses, etc. Engaging in this type of conversation allows others to notice you. If nothing else, they'll be able to ascertain that you're friendly and happy. If anything, at least, they'll get off the elevator, thinking, *Wow, that employee was nice.* I believe a lot of people miss this opportunity to show others something about their character, especially when they're not given the frequent opportunity to do so.

As a leader, I'm very observant of the actions of other, but more importantly, I understand that my actions, more than anyone, must be aligned with my professional and personal values, and should be clearly illuminated from day to day. As a leader, people look to you to help and support them in various ways. Because I wanted to learn how to be a better leader, I closely watched how leaders with far more experience responded in certain instances. Some of them set very good examples, while others fell short. Nevertheless, in each observation, a lesson was learned. I remember working for a supervisor who was a great speaker and presented himself professionally, but his actions, to me, always had a bit of negativity surrounding them. At times, he created his own problems by overreacting to situations. Based on observation, I was keenly aware of what I wanted to add to my repertoire from this leader, and what practices to keep at bay.

"Great leaders don't set out to be a leader—
they set out to make a difference. It's never
about the role, it's always about the goal."

—Lisa Haisha

ACTION STEPS:

1. Dare to travel down a path not traveled by many, but by the brave of heart.

2. Learn from everyone. Learn what to do and what not to do.

CHAPTER 6

WHEN THE GOING GETS TOUGH

"Don't be afraid of pressure. Pressure is what transforms a lump of coal into a diamond."

—Nicky Gumbel

A nyone who's in a leadership position will tell you that it isn't easy to be a leader. It takes a variety of skills to not only be effective, but also to keep your temper when under pressure. As humans, when we encounter stress or pressure, we can react in various ways. We can internalize the added pressure and become very reserved, attitudinal, grouchy, or even cool, calm, and collected. Ultimately, when pressure is applied to your already complicated and task-filled life, it can help you grow as a leader. Being able to deal with pressure in the workplace is a highly sought-after skill. If pressure at work is part of your everyday life, you'll be pleased to learn that you can do certain things to both lower the pressure and prove to others that you can handle pressure effectively. Yep, this is your time to shine, too.

For example, while I was working in a medical clinic, one patient began having breathing complications. The nurses followed all steps to troubleshoot the issue, but the patient was in distress and fainted. While the nurses tended to the patients, as the lead administrator, I had to keep everyone calm and began delegating tasks. I had someone call 911, and instructed someone else to grab the emergency kit, etc. Throughout the episode, responding in a calm manner was paramount. If I had reacted nervously, other patients and employees would have possibly followed suit or felt as though the situation wasn't handled properly, based on the response. In the end, the patient was transported to the hospital and survived. Afterwards, some patients who witnessed the incident informed me that my nurses and I did a great job handling the matter, and everyone knew what their role was. After the incident, the team met to debrief, and everyone shared their view. All team members complimented one another as we reviewed the entire incident. Clear directions and calm response to the emergency made the difference in the outcome and how it was perceived by others. Although I felt anxious during the ordeal, I had to tap into my emotional intelligence and stay focused on the outcome, which was patient and teammate safety and following policy and procedures. After the event, I took time to debrief the matter with myself. I went into my office, shut the door, and assessed my response and approach to the situation to identify if I could have done something different.

From another perspective, leaders must deal with various teammates who have different personalities and attitudes, and sometimes those perspectives travel in all different directions. Simultaneously, leaders must address each individual when they're happy, sad, up, and down. This form of applied pressure is worth noting, because it can impact the relationship between you and the team member. I remember having to speak to an employee who was very rude and not a team player but a hard worker. Although I had heard about the behavior from other team members, I also got the opportunity to witness it for myself. One team member asked a very simple question, and the person's response to the question was rather catty. After witnessing the communication, I met one-on-one with the person. Addressing a situation such as this can be stressful, if you let it, but I focused on my outcome, which was to address the behavior, the impact it had on the team, and how it could improve for the betterment of the entire team. To start the conversation, I complimented the person's work ethic and how it benefitted the team. Also, I inquired about her "why." I asked why she worked for the organization, whose goal was to care for sick individuals. I then addressed her negative behavior and how I thought it was impacting the team. I didn't know if she was going to blow a fuse at any minute, but I knew I had no choice but to take a stand and lead. I addressed the behavior that I observed and expressed how it wasn't the best response, and even provided an example of how the question could have been answered. The person explained why she provided such a response and that she didn't mean to offend anyone. As we volleyed the topic back and forth, I eventually spelled out the behavior I expected from her, and informed her that if she ever needed to discuss barriers, my door was always open. After the conversation, I followed up with the person, just to do a quick check-in, and took the same steps with team members, who stated they saw a difference in the person's communication with others. Overall, fewer complaints were received. A situation like this could have easily been blown out of proportion if we had played tit for tat and gone back and forth with one another, but I firmly believe that sometimes you have to be what I call "professionally mature" and avoid focusing on emotions that could be conveyed either internally or externally. Being professionally mature means that you can separate your professional and personal perspectives from one another. Having a mature heart means you can control your emotions and thoughts. Over the years, I had to work to overcome these challenges. It's rare that I work with someone in their twenties who has already obtained control in these areas. It's a maturation process. Emotional maturity adds solidarity to your leadership and professional lives; without it, seamless teamwork and steady leadership become difficult to maintain. But with it, you'll be able to establish a presence of respect with those you lead.

Action Steps:

1. Welcome challenges. They will help strengthen your ability to mitigate crisis.

2. Confront negativity. Don't let it fester, because it will be harder to contain.

Poker Face Them

"Remaining calm in the midst of chaos is a superpower."

—Unknown

Another way of looking at how to keep your cool under pressure is to always keep a poker face. Now, this doesn't mean you become lifeless and show no emotion toward others, but when you learn this trait, it will be difficult for others to decipher when you're angry and need a moment to yourself or when you're overwhelmed with joy.

I'll never forget when Hurricane Ike hit Houston, and the building I worked in was obliterated by the storm. The storm tore the roof off the building, which allowed the rain to pour in and destroy our technical systems. Our only point of contact was the use of our telephones, and not all of those worked. The CEO of the organization just happened to be out of the country on vacation, and the next person in charge was a deputy director who worked for the organization for about thirty years. He called a meeting with all leadership staff in the organization to discuss how we could continue operating despite the damages. There were about forty or so people at the meeting, and everyone was making suggestions and talking over everyone else. Everyone was clearly frustrated. The deputy director calmly got everyone's attention and provided some order to the meeting. He didn't try to yell over them or out-talk them; he listened and made sound suggestions. This was the poker face at its best. By the end of the meeting, a plan was put in place, and we moved forward with providing services to the community. Months after planning, a debriefing meeting was held to provide everyone an update. During the meeting, one of the deputy's cohorts gave him kudos for how he handled such a catastrophic situation and was able to get everyone focused and working together. Since I was able to observe the poker face concept at work, firsthand, it's one example that has stuck out to me over the years, and I've never forgotten it.

Being able to handle pressure surfaces when leading others, but one must know how to handle and respond to such pressures. Organizations today are focused on meeting metrics and making quotas, which can be stressful, in and of itself. I had a conversation with a close friend because I was unhappy about some of the dynamics taking place at a particular job. It always felt like there was so much pressure on meeting metrics and, at the same time, there were numerous call-ins from employees and there wasn't readily available personnel available to help fill vacant shifts. When incidents like this occurred, I would become very frustrated, but I knew I had to keep a poker face and find someone to cover the shift so teammates and clients wouldn't be impacted. Sometimes, I was able to work it out, and other times, I couldn't, but the poker face remained. When you're a leader, people will observe you more to see how you handle and respond to various situations. During these times, you, as a leader, have the opportunity to assess your ability to internalize pressure and come out shining like a diamond when it is all said and done.

Action Steps:

1. Keep your composure at all times and simply lead.

2. Positive energy in, positive energy out. Negative energy in, and negative energy out. You choose!

Sharing the Wealth

"The first rule of management is delegation. Don't try and do everything yourself because you can't."

—Anthea Turner

As I noted in Chapter 3, "You Are What You Do," a project manager, front-line manager, or executive isn't a superhero. You have to accept the fact that you're not capable of doing it all. Instead of micromanaging those around you, or doing it all yourself, which is impossible, pay attention to delegating certain responsibilities to those who report to you, and then trust them to do the job on their own. Stress can instantly be relieved by sharing the load. It doesn't mean that you assign a task and don't follow up to ensure the task is completed correctly; following up is a must. Nevertheless, when tasks begin to pile up and you can't realistically figure out how you can accomplish the tasks by yourself, it's time to have a meeting of the minds to delegate tasks. Three of the most effective stress managers are prioritization, organization, and planning. Similarly, effective techniques include clarifying roles, defining expectations, completing jobs ahead of time, and proactively managing project schedules. Also helpful is sharpening your focus. In both your personal and professional lives, the most time and effort should be given to the most important priorities.

Leaders must know when and what to delegate. When you know where you're going and you believe in your strategy, you'll embrace the help of others to see it succeed. Your staff also wants to succeed. Getting them involved and holding them accountable shows them you care about their development. Not having a plan that you believe in shows them that no one is steering the boat! When you have employees who are good, dedicated, and hungry to succeed, depriving them of taking on some or most of the important duties is an unproductive and demoralizing way to use your most important resource. By learning to delegate effectively, you get much more accomplished (many times by people who can do it better than you) and you reserve your time and focus for the high-level strategic tasks. Extending some of your authority to those who are capable of learning from it extends your power as a leader and is one of the most valued development activities you can engage in.

Throughout my career, I have run into instances when some leaders simply didn't like to delegate tasks because they felt like someone else would do a more effective job than they could and somehow end up taking their position. You may think this sounds preposterous, but it's true! When leaders are selfish and don't delegate, this lets me know they don't trust others and can't effectively lead. In one instance, I remember having a conversation with a leader in a Fortune 500 company who shared that he didn't like to delegate tasks because he had to continuously follow up with others to ensure they were doing the tasks correctly, and it simply took too much time. I responded by validating his point but disagreeing with him, as I shared the importance of delegating tasks. When managers gain confidence in their delegation skills, they begin to see better results from the employees with these effectively delegated tasks. The benefits go beyond the expected outcomes of the job, yielding powerful benefits for the managers, the employees, and the team.

- Benefits for the leader: saves time, helps you achieve more, increases your value to focus on strategic issues.

- Benefits for employees: aids skill development, boosts self-esteem, enhances job interest.

- Benefits for the team: increases efficiency, increases flexibility, enhances teamwork, balances workloads, aids communication, retains good team members.

Another possible, more powerful benefit for the leader to recognize: if there are no employees on the team ready and able to take the leader's job, what's the likelihood that the person will be promoted elsewhere? Developing leadership strength on each team demonstrates the willingness and ability of the leader to prepare the organization for the future.

Action Steps:

1. Delegation is a perfect way to help leaders complete multiple tasks.

2. Delegation is a great opportunity for others to learn and build skills.

CHAPTER 7

LIKE-MINDED PEOPLE

"If you cannot see where you are going, ask someone who has been there before."

—Jnorris

Like-minded people are those whom we admire from afar and aspire to mimic one day. You speak the same language (strong work ethic, highly accountable, aspire to progress) and lead in a remarkably similar fashion, or you may even aspire to lead like someone else. For you to grow yourself as a leader, it would behoove you to find a mentor to help you. Mentoring consists of a relationship focused on supporting the growth and development of the mentee. The mentor becomes a source of wisdom, teaching, and support. They may advise on specific actions or behavioral changes in daily work. Working with a mentor provides innumerable benefits; not only will you receive guidance, advice, and help when trying to solve tough problems, but you'll also be able to leverage your mentor's extended network of contacts for new partnerships, employees, and clients. You may have heard or read about mentorship before, but just because you know what a mentor is, the questions may remain: how do you obtain a mentor? Do you go up to someone and ask them to be your mentor, or does the relationship sort of evolve itself over time? Well, there really isn't a sure-fire way to find your mentor, but either one of the ways I mentioned would suffice. More importantly, one can find great mentors through the inspiring people you're already interacting and working with now. They need to be people to whom you've already demonstrated your potential, who know how you think, act, communicate, and contribute. And they must like, trust, and believe in you already. Why else would they help you? They also need to believe, with absolute certainty, that you'll put to great use all their input and feedback.

I've had several mentors over the years. When I played basketball, my coach was my mentor. When I started my professional career, a few supervisors became my mentors, but one stood out from the others. The relationship with Barbara Davis was created simply from developing a solid professional relationship. I believe trust and work ethic were two factors that contributed to the relationship and allowed me to grow under her auspices. Ms. Davis worked for the organization well over thirty years, so when she spoke to me about my skill set or areas of improvement, I listened attentively and made the changes that were brought to my attention. My thinking was that I was working with someone who had worked at the organization for almost as long as I'd been alive, so she must be doing something right. Why wouldn't I listen to her advice? One thing I respected about her was that she was always respectful but honest. In one of our many one-on-one meetings, she shared that she thought my emails could have been written better. She said, "You're working on your Ph.D., but you're not writing at a Ph.D. level." After she made that candid statement, she mentioned that some parts of my attire weren't professional, and provided suggestions. At first, I thought about disagreeing with her perspective, but, instead, I didn't get offended. I actively listened because I knew she didn't bring the issue to the fore to insult me, but to help me identify areas of improvement. During that conversation, we talked about these areas, but, at the same time, she highlighted my strengths. She shared that I was very dependable and accountable and developed solid processes that enhanced the workflow of the department. You should be able to have a solid relationship with your mentor so that trust can be developed and constructive criticism can be expressed and accepted by you to help nurture your growth. During my next evaluation, she stated, "One thing I've noticed about you is that when I suggest that you consider changing something, no matter what it is, you do just that, and Sarita, that's called growth." Naturally, I was very excited that she recognized that I adhered to her feedback, and did so without complaint.

ACTION STEPS:

1. Invest in yourself and then find someone who is willing to invest in you.

2. Be open to learning from others and receptive to constructive criticism.

BE A SMART LEADER

"We now accept the fact that learning is a lifelong process of keeping abreast of change. And the most pressing task is to teach people how to learn."

—Peter Drucker,
American management consultant, educator, author

Today's successful leaders are nimble learners: people who learn quickly, are open to the new and unfamiliar, and can find learning in all types of experiences. Without knowledge, it's hard to get far in life. Knowledge applied well becomes wisdom; this is also something leaders must have in abundance if they're to be successful. One of the best sources of knowledge is books, since they usually offer the most in-depth information on any given topic. Anyone who is inclined to immerse themselves in learning has at least one of the innate qualities it takes to be a leader. And currently, books are just one of many sources to read or study to help you build on your skill set. Actually, I would state with full confidence that with sources such as YouTube, numerous blogs, support groups, clubs, and the use of the internet in general, there are far too many resources to not stay abreast of changes, new concepts, and theories geared toward any topic. So, the question is how you want to learn. Now, you may say, "Well, I can read all the information I want, but how do I apply it?" If you worked and took a college course at the same time, you should be able to take the topics discussed in the course and apply them to your job. You may not be involved in the actual process, but maybe you witness it and remember when it was discussed in the course; for some reason, the dots start to connect. During my social work studies at the University of Houston College of Social Work, I would take concepts such as the strength-based perspective, Kurt Lewin's change theory, and identify how they fit myself, employees, or the organization in general. While working on my MBA, I would recognize the theory x and y or management by walking around (MBWA) concept and apply it accordingly. While studying for my doctoral degree, I learned to look beyond what is. Regardless if the outcomes were right or wrong, the process involved wasn't static in nature, and I could, therefore, apply the concept again, but maybe from a different angle. Apply what you've learned. You have the knowledge, so use it.

Growing up, I was a tomboy, and when I discovered my love of playing basketball, it quickly became my niche. When my mother realized that I had a knack for the game, she bought me a basketball goal at my house. I played every chance I had, but most of the time it was by myself. However, three streets over in my neighborhood was my elementary school, which had an outside basketball court. All the surrounding neighborhood and high school guys would gather to play there, and I decided to join them. Most of the time, I would be the only female playing with the guys. Was it tough to play against the guys? Heck yes, but it was the best learning experience ever. I had to work extra hard, and got injured a couple of times, too, but the basketball skills and knowledge I gained were priceless. All the grit and toughness playing street ball enhanced my high school, collegiate, and semi-pro basketball careers, not to mention my overall mental toughness.

Gaining knowledge includes learning about your industry. Read the history of your industry and do some research on what's happening today. What's true now that may not be true in the future? Also, take a closer look at your chief competitors. What are their strengths and weaknesses? When I worked for a nonprofit organization, I read a few books written by nonprofit leaders. For example, I read *From Good to Great* by Peter Drucker, *The Mentor Leader* by Coach Tony Dungy, and Stephen Covey's *The Speed of Trust*. When I worked for a for-profit organization, I read books by authors like John Maxwell and Jack Welsh, just to name a few.

Another effective way of building your knowledge is gaining knowledge from others. Spend time getting to know the people around you at work who know more than you. My dad, who had only a few years of high school education, always told me to hang around people who are smarter than me. In no way am I trying to insult your intelligence—I'm simply saying there's nothing wrong with being around people who can help you grow as a person and a leader.

Learning from various methods is something you have to do continuously to stay on top of the latest trends and catchy phrases, but, most importantly, it's how you can grow your knowledge. Developing leadership skills is one of the most powerful moves you can make to transform your professional and personal life. It's an empowering process of harnessing your natural talents to inspire others. As you work on developing leadership skills, you become more attuned to your strengths and weaknesses, which creates self-awareness and the ability to relate to others.

ACTION STEPS:

1. Challenge yourself to grow before others challenge you.

2. Surround yourself with people who are moving in the same direction as you.

3. Keep an open mind, and let fresh minds provide you with fresh ideas.

BE CONFIDENT

"No man can make you feel inferior without your consent."

—Eleanor Roosevelt

Far too many times, I remember feeling intimidated by more experienced leaders at work. I would marvel at people who were very well-spoken, and their pronunciation of every syllable was correct. I doubted myself quite often, and would say things like, "I could never present in front of an audience and use the correct verbiage. I'd be nervous. And what if I would simply stink up the gym?" Although I always considered myself to be confident, the doubt sometimes held me back. What I did to strengthen my position was, when I attended meetings with executive-level staff, I would attentively listen and ask questions to show that I was listening and/or interject a statement or present an idea that would make others say, "You made a good point; that's something we could consider," or they would disagree altogether. During these opportunities, and although still nervous at times, I worked on evolving my vocabulary daily. Every day, I would review one word and add it to my vernacular. Even if I never used it, I now knew the definition of the word and how to use it when interfacing with others. As humans, we tend to judge people by their cover and doubt a person's ability until they prove themselves. Instead of thinking of myself as little old Sarita from St. Louis, Missouri, I first had to realize that I was just as smart and capable as everyone sitting at the table. I believed in myself, and I was going to be sure that others did, too. I had to learn to value myself. This doesn't mean negate others or become selfish, but know your worth and value everything you bring to the table, because, if you're not confident, it will be reflected in everything you do. It's sort of ironic because, when I became more confident in my abilities, I soon started to quickly identify the flaws in other leaders, and some of them I truly admired. It didn't mean my level of admiration changed; they were still strong leaders. But I understood that they, too, had idiosyncrasies. Nevertheless, I focused on the changes I needed to make to continue to build my confidence and respect with leaders within the organization. If you're not confident within yourself, how can you expect others to be?

I'm not suggesting for you to be confident yet lack knowledge. Those two factors don't mesh very well, but when you are confident and willing to learn and grow, you're headed in the right direction. My competitive nature is what helped me stand when I made mistakes or a bad decision. In the fall of 2018, I delegated a task to my administrative assistant. I asked that she update the credentials of all teammates, and to be sure everyone was up to date on training. Sounds like an easy enough task, right? About two weeks later, I was hit with a surprise audit. The auditors requested to review the teammate credentials, which I knew had been updated by the AA because I assigned the task two weeks ago. I requested that she forward the spreadsheet to me. Upon receipt of the spreadsheet, I didn't open it to review it; I simply forwarded it to the auditors, who reviewed it and brought to my attention that it wasn't completed. At that point, I looked rather dumbfounded and embarrassed, opened the spreadsheet, and, to my surprise, it had not been completed. I felt so outdone and ashamed. All I could do was let them know I would update the spreadsheet and have it completed in a couple of days. I worked until about midnight on the spreadsheet, got assistance the next day from a few team members, and we were able to complete the spreadsheet within the expected timeframe. This was truly a lesson learned. The first thing I did was assess myself, and right away grappled with the fact that I was at fault because I delegated a task but didn't follow up and didn't review the spreadsheet before I submitted it. I then followed up with my administrative assistant to discuss the assignment and expectation. Although still feeling embarrassed, I immediately decided that, if I could control it, an instance like that would never happen again. I pulled myself up by the bootstraps and worked harder to improve systems and processes. A month after the audit, the auditors made another visit and reviewed the plan of correction. At that point, all errors had been corrected and the clinical scores were higher than they had ever been. This incident could have gone drastically left if I had given up and acted as though the errors didn't matter. Instead, I decided to take a stance and work harder to make improvements. Was it easy fixing the errors? Of course not, but I was determined to not let others doubt my abilities to lead. I had to be strong and confident. It simply wasn't a choice.

Self-confidence is an essential part of leadership. A leader with self-confidence thinks positively about the future and is willing to take the risks necessary to achieve their personal and professional goals. A leader who lacks self-confidence, on the other hand, is less likely to feel that they can achieve their goals, with a negative perspective about themselves and what they hope to gain in life—attitudes that are destructive to leadership and success.

The good news is that self-confidence is something you can improve and build. Not every leader is born with natural self-confidence, but you can build confidence by addressing the self-doubt. Identify the doubt, seek to understand why it exists, and work to resolve and tune it out entirely. As I stated before, don't be afraid to make mistakes, because mistakes are sometimes the best teachers. Surround yourself with optimistic but realistic people. Understand that everyone isn't going to be in your corner, so having people support and encourage you can make a world of difference.

Per my example, don't let one wrong turn, or even a few of them, make you think you don't have what it takes to achieve your goals and reach your success. Take pride in your abilities. Pride feeds the soul; it helps you recognize and appreciate who you are and what you can accomplish.

Sometimes it's the motivation we need when things get tough.

Lastly, lead from within. Confidence is as important to leadership as oxygen is to breathing. If you're lacking in confidence, you're lacking in influence. Most people think leadership is about being the smartest person in the room, but what I've learned from my own experience and from observing hundreds of senior-level executives is that there's incredible power in being able to accept that you're not that person, at least not yet. But if you have the confidence and patience, you can be one of the smartest persons in the room one day.

"A leader can inspire a group only if he himself is filled with confidence and hope of success."

—Floyd V. Filson

ACTION STEPS:

1. Don't let others define who you are as a leader.

2. Confidence is what you think you can do, not what others think you can do.

3. Present how you want to be perceived by others.

CHAPTER 8

CAN PEOPLE RELATE TO YOU?

"All good leaders are connectors. They relate well and make people feel confident about themselves and their leader."

—John Maxwell

I know this book is about claiming your place as a leader, but have you ever dated someone and you simply didn't find them to be compatible, for whatever reason? It could have been the way they laughed, dressed, or they were rude or disrespectful, but at the end of the date, there was no connection. The same frame of mind could be true with a leader who cannot connect with the people they lead. You must make sure you can relate, on some level, to the people you lead. If I'm interested in knowing how a certain leader leads, I'll ask around. Each person has their own perception of reality, and they're forthcoming most of the time. Before I worked for my mentor, Barbara Davis, I asked others what it was like to work with her, and I received varied responses. Some said she was tough, some said she was down to earth, and some stated she was a "nice person" to work for. I immediately thought, *Well, she must be a good leader.* When I interviewed with her, she asked me what I had heard about her, and I repeated what I heard. She asked me what I thought about what I was told. I replied, "I heard you were tough, but I'm not afraid of work." She responded, "Great, then we should get along just fine." As I grew to know her over the years, we always talked about our families, life goals, and topics in the news. Because it was easy to relate to her through our conversations and job tasks, a rapport was developed.

In the same vein, I had a supervisor whose conversation focused on the stock market and playing golf. In my mind, I was thinking, *I'm here working for fifteen bucks an hour and trying to be sure I can feed my daughter, and you're talking about the stock market.* I listened attentively and would just smile and nod my head as if I were interested in the topic. Being relatable resonates with me and how I parent my children. When we converse about dating, high school or college, and life in general, I use language they can relate to, and I monitor my tone. I take these intentional steps because I want them to be comfortable sharing information with me, and I want them to be open with me. Most of the time, it works. As a leader, you must recognize there's a time for work on a professional level, a time for semi-work, or when you relate on a personal level. Employees feel happy when managers connect with them on a personal level. They are more apt to come to work, face challenges with you, and constantly strive to help take their organization to the next level. I've worked with various generations of employees, and what I often notice is that the millennials need a bit more attention compared to a baby boomer. So, as a leader, you have to adapt your conversation according to whom you're talking to and what you're talking about.

Another point to note is that leaders need to know whether or not their team members are happy with their jobs. Don't make your employees feel ignored or left out. Believe me, if they feel ignored, they will hardly work instead of work hard. Unless and until they feel themselves indispensable to the organization, they will never take things seriously. In such cases, individuals may be in the office just to receive their paychecks and treat work as a necessary burden. This type of employee is mostly never a good fit for the culture, but the way you relate to the employee can possibly change their attitude. Leaders need to understand that employees need to be appreciated for them to perform consistently. Actually, *The 5 Languages of Appreciation in the Workplace* by Dr. Chapman and Dr. White gives you practical steps to make any workplace environment more encouraging and productive.

Problems arise when managers don't acknowledge the hard work of employees. Remember, you're not paid for just sitting in your office and passing on instructions to your team members. Some managers don't even know their team members' names. Sit with your team members regularly to know them, evaluate their work, and provide feedback. As a manager, it's your responsibility to guide your team members and help them achieve their targets within the stipulated timeframe. Employees feel happy and proud to be a part of the organization when their performances are noticed. Wouldn't you? For example, I hired a clinician who needed to be trained by a lead clinician. From the time the person started training, the top-level clinician never spoke to the new hire. In fact, she didn't acknowledge her for about three weeks (I was totally unaware at the time). When she finally acknowledged her, it was too late. Between the two of them, the so-called clinical leader made no attempts to get to know the new employee. One day, the new hire came into my office and was very upset. She stated that the lead clinician acted like she didn't want to help her. I intervened to try to determine the issue, but the new hire left a couple of days later and never returned. I couldn't believe we lost an experienced employee because the lead clinician lacked leadership skills and didn't try to get to know the new hire. Shame on us!

Leaders must be able to show others they have a flexible personality. This means they can relate to people on different levels. They should be able to hold a conversation with everyone, from the person at the information booth to the janitors, and from information technology all the way up to the executive-level employees. When leaders are versatile in their abilities to comingle with people of different ethnicities, they really are opening the doors for them to learn more about individuals who are different. A habit that I've formed is when I walk into a conference or business meeting, I intentionally sit with people I don't know, or maybe someone I work with, but I've never held a conversation with them. I introduce myself and start small conversations about work, the meeting, the weather, or whatever it takes to open the door of communication. My goal is to learn something about them and vice versa—no more, no less. But the next time I see them in the building, I'll speak to them by name and may possibly learn more about the person over time. Even if I don't see the person often, at least the person is aware of me, and that's the key, regardless of what position is held. Why would anyone want to follow someone who thinks they're high and mighty and knows everything? I certainly don't. In fact, those types of people turn me off very quickly, although I don't let it show, and it's a mental note scribbled in my brain. The essence of leadership is getting people who inherently know more about the nuts and bolts of whatever it is you're leading better than you ever will to follow your lead and vision.

ACTION STEPS:

1. Be versatile. Learn a little something about everything.

2. Be open to differences in people and willing to accept them.

Laugh out Loud and Have Fun at Work

"Laughter is a bodily exercise, precious to health."

—Aristotle

While playing professional basketball for the St. Louis RiverQueens, we were on a road trip and someone kept making me laugh. The owner of the team, while listening from afar, said, "You have a very distinct laugh, but you are always laughing and I like that." I'm not sure if what she stated was a compliment or not, but it was true. During my high school days, a reporter asked my mother about me, and she was quoted as saying, "Sarita always laughs; if she isn't laughing, something is wrong." I didn't realize I had such a jovial spirit at the time, but, looking back, I laughed a lot, and, to this day, I still do. Laughter is good for the soul and can truly make a difference in your outlook on life, but please note: it starts from the inside out. If you're at work and always grumpy, that's exactly how you'll be perceived by others. Most recently, for "Boss's Day" one employee gave me a card that had the word joy written on it and a little passage that said, "She lives joyfully not because her circumstances were joyful, but because she was joyful" by Dieter F. Vohtdorf. What a very nice statement that spoke to her perception of me.

Also, tasteful humor is a key to success at work. "Humor, by its nature, tends to have an edge to it, so people typically tone it down at work," says Laura Vanderkam, author of *What the Most Successful People Do at Work* and *What the Most Successful People Do Before Breakfast*. "It's hard to do well and easy to do badly. Plus, we all tend to take ourselves way too seriously." Leaders with humor can build stronger cultures, unleash more creativity, and even negotiate better deals. "We hear from young leaders about the incredible pressure of being the face of their organization," says Aaker. "Many struggle because they hold on to the false dichotomy between bringing humor and taking your work seriously. The right balance of gravity and levity gives power to both." Leaders who favor a teasing style (i.e., saying whatever amuses them without worrying about how it affects others, or using humorous sparring as a way to build relationships) can alienate those who are the total opposite.

Your sense of humor is a muscle. It gets stronger the more you use it. Incorporating levity, not just in presentations but also in casual conversations, certain emails, or even your out-of-office reply message, can be appropriate. If you're sending out a mundane communication where levity wouldn't be out of place, consider dropping in an amusing comment. When public speaking, reference funny things that happened or jokes made earlier by you or by others. Never punch down by targeting a subordinate. Keep it light. When employees can relate to their leaders, it lightens the tension caused by other factors in the workplace and can even make the job enjoyable. "Good comedy is a conspiracy. Create an in-group," advise Peter McGraw and Joel Warner in *The Humor Code*, a book about what makes funny things funny. Being "in" on the inside jokes can make team members feel like they're part of the group.

Owen Lynch, in his article "Kitchen Antics: The Importance of Humor and Maintaining Professionalism at Work" in the *Journal of Applied Communication Research*, found that humor "draws people together based on their shared understandings and provides ingroups with a common form of expression." That is, we communicate our shared experiences through jokes. "Humor begets bonding; in return, bonding begets more ingroup humor." Although they exist and we all must do it at some point, I would rather not attend stuffy meetings with stuffy people, but that's just me. A good punch line interjected here or there, allowing everyone to laugh together, helps build the camaraderie of the team, and it's a tactic I use to this day. At one job, daily huddles were needed to discuss the day's events, or just to have a quick check-in with everyone. During this time, I presented jovially and started and ended the meeting with a funny remark. What I noticed over time was that other employees would add their funny comments throughout the meeting, too, and I soon realized that the employees felt comfortable enough that they could say something funny, and it was okay to do so when the opportunity presented itself. The ability to laugh is a gift, and you should utilize it in a professional and thoughtful manner.

ACTION STEPS:

1. Laughter is good for the soul at work, if it's in good context.

2. Laughter is contagious. Encourage others to have a sense of humor.

BE UNDERSTANDING, BUT HOLD PEOPLE ACCOUNTABLE

"Accountability breeds response-ability."

—Stephen R. Covey

One of my favorite quotes by Stephen Covey from his book *The 7 Habits of Highly Effective People* is, "First seek to understand, then seek to be understood." I cannot tell you how many times this quote has raced through my mind while meeting with one of my employees to address an issue. Most often, when someone doesn't abide by the policy or may not be the best employee, we're quick to rush to judge the situation even before we know what occurred. When I have to confront an employee, I'll let them explain their perspective, and then we converse about what was right or wrong, but at the end of the conversation, the policies and expectations must be followed, and those steps are spelled out to the employee and documented. Regardless of the outcome, as a leader, you can't always jump to conclusions; you must first be willing to actively listen to get a better understanding of the matter. Humans are extraordinary, complex creatures. We long for understanding, and we instantly sniff out when someone is trying to understand or just being patronizing. Your job as a leader is to really hear what people are saying, not what you want to hear or what you think you heard.

Leaders must be understanding when employees are dealing with "life" ordeals. At times, people hit bumps in the road and may experience things such as divorce, death, health issues, depression, or just good old-fashioned stress that hits us out of nowhere. Yes, as a leader you must deal with the whole person—that includes the good and the bad.

So, if you're empathetic, you can apply your awareness of other people's feelings and understand how those feelings affect their needs. When you're an empathetic leader, you're aware of how these feelings impact the other person's perception. This is irrespective of whether you agree with them or can relate to them or not. You can appreciate what another person is going through when you display empathy. An employee met with me about her mother, who was very ill, and she was having a tough time dealing with it because her mother lived in one state and she lived in another. While the employee shared the information, I made eye contact, attentively listened, and nodded my head to show her that she had my full attention. I didn't check my email or answer the phone when it rang; I stopped working and listened. When the employee finished explaining the ordeal, I validated her concerns and explained a few options she had that would allow her to balance work and personal life. Additionally, I informed her that if there was anything I could to assist her, I would do my best. The reason I made that statement is because I wanted the employee to know that I would support her to the best of my ability within the means of the job.

On the other hand, you'll encounter people who don't want to follow policy and procedures and will always try to take advantage of the system. People will suck the life out of an organization and abuse the sick, late, and FMLA policies, just to name a few. You'll notice these individuals right away because they'll have exhausted accrued leave time, have a multitude of excuses for being late, and their work ethic will be subpar. Nevertheless, you should have policies on your side that help support addressing the identified behaviors. The key to handling behavior of this sort is to address it right away, and when it becomes problematic, make sure you use the company policy as your leverage. When your decisions are aligned with policy, you can minimize any possible mistakes that can come back to bite you. Responding to instances like this doesn't mean you're not being understanding. It just means that you're holding people accountable who need it. I'll never forget a young man who literally begged me to hire him. He presented himself very professionally and had some experience working in the health field. I hired him, and while he was in training, he would often show up late to work. This position entailed working long hours, and the day started at 5 a.m. Five in the morning is incredibly early for some, especially if you may not go to sleep until midnight. He was a fair worker, at that, but the issue with being tardy soon became problematic for team members who had to help him out when he ran behind, and they had enough. I met with him to discuss the issue of tardiness, followed policy, and issued a verbal warning. During our discussion, I took the time to focus on the accomplishments he had made to date, but I still held him accountable and explained that when he was late, it impacted the workday for him and the entire team. After our first discussion, he continued to be late, and we had another meeting. Eventually, he asked, "Do you know how hard it is to wake up at four in the morning to get ready for work?" Admittedly, I was taken aback because this person hounded me to hire them and was aware of the work hours when hired. After a few more write-ups, he was dismissed. I understand that people need a job, but they must be willing to uphold their part of the bargain. As a leader, you'll have to make tough decisions, but be sure to follow company policy and do what's best for the greater good.

ACTION STEPS:

1. Accountability should not be seen as a punitive action, but, rather, a method to raise the bar of others' performance.

2. Let people determine their own fate.

CHAPTER 9

LOOK INSIDE YOURSELF

"Try not to become a man of success, but a man of value."

—Albert Einstein

When was the last time you took a good, hard look at yourself and assessed your world? You could conduct a SWOT assessment by gauging your Strengths, Weaknesses, Opportunities, and Threats. You may or may not be amazed at the outcomes, but assessing oneself is a powerful tool that can help you better understand where you want to go and what you need to do to get there. This path includes how you'll continue to grow as a leader. Leadership is a topic that's easily spoken about but can be challenging to ascertain if you don't apply yourself. Growth in leadership is mandatory, not optional. If we fail to grow, it's not a matter of just staying where we are—we become stagnant and fall further and further behind.

Growing as a leader requires that we give up familiar things, take new steps, and do things in new ways. Those actions are what change is made of. The reward lies not in what we get from growth, but in what we become because of our growth.

Here are some daily habits you can begin to grow as a leader:

1. Develop a repertoire of skills. To be the best leader you're capable of being, you need to constantly be mastering new competencies, instead of relying on the skills you already have under your belt. Growing leaders are constantly updating and expanding their skills and knowledge.

    Earlier in the book, I referenced the importance of building your craft, but attending trainings, reading, and researching information, and your willingness to take on additional assignments at work can greatly enhance your skill set. Also, college degrees help, as well. Showing others that you're willing to better yourself by furthering your education is an indicator that you want to learn, better yourself, and grow.

2. Learn through your experiences. The more you experience, the more you know. That means that even the most difficult challenges present an opportunity to engage in those experiences, learn the lessons they hold, and apply your new knowledge to whatever comes next.

As the adage goes, "experience is a good teacher." For me, it has been one of the best teachers. After the numerous times I failed, got up, and failed again, and the times I excelled at various tasks without being in a leadership position, I always assessed the matter and focused on the learning points. What did I learn and what could I have done differently are two questions I often pose to myself—do you?

3. Challenge your comfort zone. It's tempting to lull yourself into always doing the same things in the same ways with the same people at the same time with the same results. But there's no room in that picture for stretching yourself to become better. Get comfortable being uncomfortable, because that's how you grow.

Being comfortable is something we all love. Once we do things a certain way repeatedly, it becomes second nature and you become a subject matter expert. After you've learned everything, do you continue to push yourself to grow, or do you remain mundane and comfortable? Taking on tasks outside or within your pay grade is a great way to grow. Similarly, having a good friend or mentor to help push you is of utmost important, too. When others hold you accountable, you tend to respond a bit differently than if you were only accountable to yourself. We all need a push sometimes in our lives. An adage that I hold near and dear to my heart today is "familiarity breeds content." Can you grow with simply being content?

4. Focus on the present to positively affect the future. When you're stuck in the past, it can be hard to get unstuck; but when you're focused on the present, you know that everything you do today will affect the future. Growing leaders know that the present is the foundation for the future.

   Let bygones be bygones. If your past consists of regretful decisions, mistakes, or failure, that's okay because it's part of life and part of the growing process. Sometimes our past can hold us back, but when you're confident within yourself, regardless of what anyone else thinks, you're on your way to becoming a great leader.

5. Set the bar high. Leaders who are serious about growth are always raising the bar for themselves, not just for others. They keep the bar high and do everything they can to consistently reach it.

   Setting your own standards is a great way to elevate your presence. If you don't have standards, you'll settle for most things. When everyone else is traveling east, don't be afraid to travel west. Step out on faith and dare to be different.

6. Look within. When you first start in a position of leadership, you're more concerned with your external qualities; but as you grow in leadership, you rediscover that leading is an internal quality. To lead outwardly, you first must learn to lead from within.

   If you don't lead from within, others will be able to recognize it right away. Leading from within allows you to be more genuine, empathetic, and real with others. When others understand your "why" and it shows in the way you lead, you stand a better chance of building strong followership.

Would Others Want to Follow Your Lead?

Skills you learn as a follower are applied when you become a leader. All leaders are followers, but not all followers are leaders. The role of a follower isn't a simple one. It doesn't just mean following directions or blindly accepting everything a leader says. Good followership is characterized by active participation in the pursuit of organizational goals. In many cases, this means working independently, being accountable for your actions, and taking ownership of necessary tasks. Self-check: do you see yourself as a good follower?

Regardless of how you answered the question, the point that should be noted is that followership is just as important as leadership. If a leader doesn't know how to follow, then how can they lead? The ability to follow takes skills, just as it does to lead. Followership is all about interacting in a skillful way with your leadership to benefit both you and your organization. Learning how to be a great follower is a requirement to becoming a truly great leader.

Followership has real value. Followership has an unbreakable bond with leadership, yet we neither notice nor appreciate it. We fail to mention that the reason we have great leaders is that we have great followers.

The likes of **Oprah Winfrey, Jeff Bezos, and Martin Luther King Jr.** didn't achieve their fame on their efforts alone. Behind them were committed and dedicated workers who assisted them all the way. In the same way, no best-selling author will emerge without numerous voracious readers. A great coach is noticed because they have talented athletes who work hard. Also, exceptional students make an award-winning educator and faculty. When you become a good follower, you learn how to pay attention to people's opinions, consider their input, and work with emotional intelligence. One who hasn't been an excellent follower cares less about other people's needs, or doesn't even think of asking for their opinion. They tend to consider employees as being under them and as people meant to serve them and provide their needs. Those who don't value followership won't value others, too. Those who have value and regard for followership become the best of leaders. This is because they care about the people following them and are willing to show it. They know that they have limits as leaders and, thus, appreciate the ability of their followers to either make or break them. Being a good follower is the beginning of becoming a good leader. The purpose of leadership isn't to have people around you to cater to your needs. It's about finding out the potential of your team and doing your best to maximize these potentials as you seek to achieve a common goal.

At the same time, just because a leader leads doesn't mean they still can't follow; they may just do it in a very different way. Followers are not inferior to their leaders, and leaders are not superior to their followers. Leaders don't always have extra information or knowledge that their followers don't have access to. Leaders don't live in an alternate universe; they're flawed human beings, just like their followers. Followers must take direction, but they have an underlying obligation to the enterprise to do so only when the direction is ethical and proper. The key is having the judgment to know the difference between a directive that your leader gives on how to proceed that you don't agree with and a directive that's utterly wrong. No one disputes that good judgment is critical to be a good leader. It's just as important in the follower. Show enough good judgment as a follower and you usually end up getting a shot at being the leader. A line that I've always liked about judgment is: "Good judgment comes from experience; experience comes from bad judgment."

If you were assigned a leadership position today, would you follow you? It's not a trick question, and there isn't a right or wrong answer; nevertheless, an answer will come. The answer is totally up to you and how well you prepare yourself for your first or fifth leadership position. No matter your walk of life, you can learn to become a solid leader, but first, you must believe in yourself and your abilities. Your ability to have a greater impact on the lives and careers of others awaits you, but what steps will you take when the opportunity presents itself? Are you prepared at this very moment? If the answer is no, just know that it's never too late to gird yourself with knowledge and skills to become an effective leader. If the answer is yes, continue to enhance your skills so that, together as leaders, we can continue to make a difference and help others reach their full potential, just as others have invested into us.

"Leaders instill in their people a hope for success and a belief in themselves. Positive leaders empower people to accomplish their goals."

—Unknown

REFERENCES

Chapman, G. D, & White, P. E. (2012). *The 5 Languages of Appreciation in the Workplace: Empowering by Encouraging People.* Northfield.

Covey, S, (1989). *The 7 Habits of Highly Effective People: Powerful Lessons in Personal Change.*

James, K. and Posner, B. (2011). *Credibility: How Leaders Gain and Lose It. Why People Demand It.* Jossey-Bass.

Lombardi, V. (2001). *What It Takes to Be #1: Vince Lombardi on Leadership.* McGraw-Hill

Maxwell, J.C. (1998), *The 21 Irrefutable Laws of Leadership: Follow Them and People will Follow You.* Thomas Nelson.

Maxwell, J.C. (2000). *The 21 Most Powerful Minutes in a Leader's Day: Revitalize Your Spirit and Empower Your Leadership.* Thomas Nelson,

McGraw, P. and Warner, J. (2014). *The Humor Code: A Global Search For What Makes Things Funny.* Simon and Schuster

Owens, H. L. (2009) *Kitchen Antics: The Importance of Humor and Maintaining Professionalism at Work.*

Tzu, L. (1772) The Art of War. Translated by John Minford. New York: Viking. 2002.

Vanderkam, L. (2012). *What the Most Successful People Do Before*

Breakfast: A Short Guide to Making over Your Mornings—and Life. Goodreads.

Welch, J (2006). *The Speed of Trust: The One Thing That Changes Everything.* Simon and Schuster.

ABOUT THE AUTHOR

Sarita Wesley, Ph.D., LMSW has always tried to learn from her experiences on her path to enhancing her leadership skills as a collegiate athlete, to working in the nonprofit and profit sectors, and teaching various leadership and management courses to students over the past ten years. The knowledge she has ascertained is shared in *Step Up Your Game*. Dr. Wesley provides insight, encouragement, and steps to help you tackle self-doubt or any other challenge you may face to ultimately grow your leadership skills.

You can be a better leader—
Whatever your background, age, or field of endeavor.

—Pat Williams

THANK YOU FOR
READING MY BOOK!

I really appreciate all of your feedback,
and I love hearing what you have to say.

I need your input to make the next version
of this book and my future books better.

Please leave me an honest review on Amazon
letting me know what you thought of the book.

Thanks so much!

Sarita Wesley, Ph.D., LMSW

www.ingramcontent.com/pod-product-compliance
Lightning Source LLC
Chambersburg PA
CBHW071606200326
41519CB00021BB/6892